Dedication

To all those who ever struggled with learning a foreign language and to Wolfgang Karfunkel

Also by Yatir Nitzany

Conversational Spanish Quick and Easy

....

Conversational French Quick and Easy

....

Conversational Italian Quick and Easy

....

Conversational Portuguese Quick and Easy

....

Conversational German Quick and Easy

....

Conversational Dutch Quick and Easy

....

Conversational Norwegian Quick and Easy

....

Conversational Danish Quick and Easy

....

Conversational Russian Quick and Easy

....

Conversational Ukrainian Quick and Easy

....

Conversational Bulgarian Quick and Easy

....

Conversational Polish Quick and Easy

....

Conversational Hebrew Quick and Easy

....

Conversational Yiddish Quick and Easy

....

Conversational Armenian Quick and Easy

....

Conversational Arabic Quick and Easy

....

Conversational Spanish Quick and Easy

The Most Innovative Technique to Learn the Spanish Language

Part II

YATIR NITZANY

Translated by:
Semadar Mercedes Friedman

Interior Design:
Menachem Otto

Foreword

About Myself

For many years I struggled to learn Spanish, and I still knew no more than about twenty words. Consequently, I was extremely frustrated. One day I stumbled upon this method as I was playing around with word combinations. Suddenly, I came to the realization that every language has a certain core group of words that are most commonly used and, simply by learning them, one could gain the ability to engage in quick and easy conversational Spanish.

I discovered which words those were, and I narrowed them down to three hundred and fifty that, once memorized, one could connect and create one's own sentences. The variations were and are *infinite*! By using this incredibly simple technique, I could converse at a proficient level and speak Spanish. Within a week, I astonished my Spanish-speaking friends with my newfound ability. The next semester I registered at my university for a Spanish language course, and I applied the same principles I had learned in that class (grammar, additional vocabulary, future and past tense, etc.) to those three hundred and fifty words I already had memorized, and immediately I felt as if I had grown wings and learned how to fly.

At the end of the semester, we took a class trip to San José, Costa Rica. I was like a fish in water, while the rest of my classmates were floundering and still struggling to converse. Throughout the following months, I again applied the same principle to other languages—French, Portuguese, Italian, and Arabic, all of which I now speak proficiently, thanks to this very simple technique.

This method is by far the fastest way to master quick and easy conversational language skills. There is no other technique that compares to my concept. It is effective, it worked for me, and it will work for you. Be consistent with my program, and you too will succeed the way I and many, many others have.

Table of Contents

Introduction to the Program

In the first book, you were taught the 350 most useful words in the Spanish language, which, once memorized, could be combined in order for you to create your own sentences. Now, with the knowledge you have gained, you can use those words in Conversational Spanish Quick and Easy Part 2 and Part 3, in order to supplement the 350 words that you've already memorized. This combination of words and sentences will help you master the language to even greater proficiency and quicker than with other courses.

The books that comprise Parts 2 and 3 have progressed from just vocabulary and are now split into various categories that are useful in our everyday lives. These categories range from travel to food to school and work, and other similarly broad subjects. In contrast to various other methods, the topics that are covered also contain parts of vocabulary that are not often broached, such as the military, politics, and religion. With these more unusual topics for learning conversational languages, the student can learn quicker and easier. This method is flawless and it has proven itself time and time again.

If you decide to travel to Spain or Latin America, then this book will help you speak the Spanish language.

This method has worked for me and thousands of others. It surpasses any other language-learning method system currently on the market today.

This book, Part 2, specifically deals with practical aspects concerning travel, camping, transportation, city living, entertainment such as films, food including vegetables and fruit, shopping, family including grandparents, in-laws, and stepchildren, human anatomy, health, emergencies, and natural disasters, and home situations.

The sentences within each category can help you get by in other countries.

In relation to travel, for example, you are given sentences about food, airport necessities such as immigration, and passports. Helpful phrases include, "Where is the immigration and passport control inside the airport?" and "I want to order a bowl of cereal and toast with jelly." For flights there are informative combinations such as, "There is a long line of passengers in the terminal because of the delay on the runway." When arriving in another country options for what to say include, "We want to hire a driver for the tour. However, we want to pay with a credit card instead of cash" and, "On which street is the car-rental agency?"

When discussing entertainment in another country and in a new language, you are provided with sentences and vocabulary that will help you interact with others. You can discuss art galleries and watching foreign films. For example, you may need to say to friends, "I need subtitles if I watch a foreign film" and, 'The mystery-suspense genre films are usually good movies'. You can talk about your own filming experience in front of the camera.

The selection of topics in this book is much wider than in ordinary courses. By including social issue such as incarceration, it will help you to engage with more people who speak the language you are learning.

Part 3 will deal with vocabulary and sentences relevant to indoor matters such as school and the office, but also a variety of professions and sports.

.

The Spanish Language

Spanish originated in Spain, and it closely resembles Portuguese, as both are Latin in their derivation and, therefore, Romance languages. The Spanish language was spread during the 1500s by Spanish colonialists coming from Spain to South America. Since then, the language has grown and is now the fourth most-spoken language in the world. Spanish is still rising in popularity, as it has 98 million non-native speakers and 402 million native speakers. Don't you want to be a member of the ever-growing population of Spanish speakers? Now you can be, if you follow the simple instructions of this program.

Memorization Made Easy

There is no doubt the three hundred and fifty words in my program are the required essentials in order to engage in quick and easy basic conversation in any foreign language. However, some people may experience difficulty in the memorization. For this reason, I created Memorization Made Easy. This memorization technique will make this program so simple and fun that it's unbelievable! I have spread the words over the following twenty pages. Each page contains a vocabulary table of ten to fifteen words. Below every vocabulary box, sentences are composed from the words on the page that you have just studied. This aids greatly in memorization. Once you succeed in memorizing the first page, then proceed to the second page. Upon completion of the second page, go back to the first and review. Then proceed to the third page. After memorizing the third, go back to the first and second and repeat. And so on. As you continue, begin to combine words and create your own sentences in your head. Every time you proceed to the following page, you will notice words from the previous pages will be present in those simple sentences as well, because repetition is one of the most crucial aspects in learning any foreign language. Upon completion of your twenty pages, *congratulations,* you have absorbed the required words and gained a basic, quick-and-easy proficiency and you should now be able to create your own sentences and say anything you wish in the Spanish language. This is a crash course in conversational Spanish, and it works!

Reading and Pronunciation

The pronunciation of Spanish, in comparison to the English language, is more or less the same. There are, however, a few exceptions that are listed below. Please read and familiarize yourself with the rules of Spanish pronunciation.

CE is pronounced as "se." *Él dice* is pronounced as "él di-se."

G when followed by *e* or *i* sounds like the letter *h* in English, like "hot." For example, *general* is pronounced as "he-nere-ral."

H is silent. For example, *hacer* is pronounced as acer

J is pronounced similar to the *ch* in German and in Hebrew ("loch," "channuka," and "yacht"). For example, the English word "garden", translated *jardin* in Spanish, would sound like "chardin." The sound is a little difficult to pronounce for non-Spanish speakers. Tip: pronounce as if you are coughing up phlegm in the back of your throat. The English word "job", translated *trabajo*, is pronounced as "tra-ba-cho."

Ñ is pronounced as "ny." For example, "morning," *mañana*, sounds like "ma-ny-ana."

LL is pronounced as "je." For example, "to arrive," *llegar*, sounds like "je-gar." However, in some Spanish countries, they pronounce it as "ye"; *llegar* would be pronounced as "ye-gar."

RR is hard to pronounce for non-Spanish speakers, but an easy Tip is that the pronunciation is similar to the sound of a starting car engine, "rrrrrr." "Dog," *perro*, would be pronounced as "pe-rrrr-o."

V is pronounced as "b." *Victor* would be pronounced as "Biktor."

Z is pronounced as "s." For example shoe, *zapato*, would be pronounced as "sapato."

TRAVEL - VIAJE

Flight - Vuelo
Airplane - Avión
Airport – Aeropuerto / **Terminal -** Terminal
Passport - Pasaporte / **Customs -** Aduanas
Take off (airplane) – Despegar / **Landing -** Aterrizaje
Gate – Puerta de embarque / Embarque
Departure - Salida / **Arrival –** Llegada
Luggage - Equipaje / **Suitcase -** Maleta
Baggage claim - Recogida de equipaje
Passenger – (Male) Pasajero / **(Female)**pasajera
Final Destination – Destino final
Boarding - Embarque
Runway - Pista
Line - Línea
Delay - Demoro
Wing - Ala

I like to travel.
Me gusta viajar.
This is a very expensive flight.
Este es un vuelo muy caro (expensive).
The airplane takes off in the morning and lands at night.
El avión despega por la mañana y aterriza por la noche.
My suitcase is at the baggage claim.
Mi maleta está en la recogida de equipaje.
We need to go to the departure gate instead of the arrival gate.
Necesitamos ir a la puerta de salida en lugar de la puerta de llegada.
There is a long line of passengers in the terminal because of a delay on the runway.
Hay una larga línea de pasajeros en el terminal, por la demora en la pista.
What is your final destination?
¿Cuál es tu destino final?
I don't like to sit above the wing of the airplane.
No me gusta sentarme encima del la ala del avión.
The flight takes off at 3pm, but the boarding commences at 2:20pm.
El vuelo despega a las 3:00pm en punto., pero el embarque comienza a las 2:20pm.
Do I need to check in my luggage?
¿Tengo que registrar mi equipaje?
Where is the passport control inside the airport?
¿Dónde está el control de pasaportes en el aeropuerto?
I am almost finished at customs.
Casi termino con las aduanas.

International flights – Vuelos internacionales
Domestic flights – Vuelos domésticos
First class – Primera clase
Business class – Clase ejecutiva
Economy class – Clase economía
Direct flight - Vuelo directo
Round trip - Viaje ida y vuelta
One-way flight - Vuelo de una dirección
Return flight - Vuelo de regreso
Flight attendant - Azafata /auxiliar de vuelo
Layover - Escala / **Connection** - Conexión
Reservation - Reservaciones / reservas
Security check – Control de seguridad
Checked bags - Maletas facturadas / **Carry on bag** - Maleta de mano
Business trip - Viaje de negocios
Check in counter – Mostrador de facturación
Travel agency - Agencia de viajes
Temporary visa – Visa temporal / **Permanent visa** – Visa permanente
Country – País

The flight attendant told me to go to the check in counter.
La azafata me dijo que vaya al mostrador de facturación.
For international flights you must be at the airport at least three hours before the flight.
Para vuelos internacionales, debe de llegar al aeropuerto tres horas antes del vuelo.
For a domestic flight, I need to arrive at the airport at least two hours before the flight.
Para un vuelo doméstico, necesito llegar al aeropuerto al menos dos horas antes del vuelo.
Business class is usually cheaper than first class.
La clase ejecutiva en general (usually) es más barata (cheaper) que la primera clase.
Through the travel agency, the one-way ticket was cheaper than the round-trip ticket.
A través de la agencia de viajes, el boleto de una dirección era más barato que el boleto de ida y vuelta.
I prefer a direct flight without a layover.
Prefiero un vuelo directo sin escala.
I must make reservations for my return flight.
Tengo que reservar mi vuelo de regreso.
Why do I need to remove my shoes at the security check?
¿Por qué tengo que quitar mis zapatos en el control de seguridad?
I have three checked bags and one carry-on.
Tengo tres maletas facturadas y una de mano.
I have to ask my travel agent if this country requires a visa.
Tengo que preguntar a mi agente de viajes si este país requiere una visa.

Trip – Viaje
Tourist - Turista / **Tourism -** Turismo
Holidays - Fiestas / **Vacations -** Vacaciones
Currency exchange - Cambio de efectivo
Port of entry - Puerto de entrada
Car rental agency - Agencia de automóviles para alquilar
Identification - Identificación
GPS - GPS
Road - La carretera
Map - Mapa
Information center - Centro de Información
Bank - Banco
Hotel – Hotel / **Motel -** Motel / **Hostel -** Hostal
Leisure - Ocio / divertimiento
Driver – (Male) Conductor/ **(Female)** conductora
Tour - Excursión
Credit - Crédito / **Cash -** Efectivo
A guide - Un guía
Ski Resort - Estación de esquí

I had an amazing trip.
Tuve un viaje asombroso (amazing).
The currency exchange counter is past the port of entry.
El mostrador (counter) de cambio de efectivo esta al pasar de la entrada.
There is a lot of tourism during the holidays and vacations.
Hay mucho turismo durante las fiestas y las vacaciones.
Where is the car-rental agency?
¿Dónde está la agencia de automóviles para alquilar?
You need to show your identification whenever checking at a hotel
Tienes que mostrar tu identificación cada vez que tu te registras en un hotel.
It's more convenient to use the GPS on the roads instead of a map.
Usar el GPS es más conveniente que usar un mapa en las carreteras.
Why is the information center closed today?
¿Por qué el centro de información está cerrado hoy?
When I am in a new country, I go to the bank before I go to the hotel.
Cuando estoy en un nuevo país, voy al banco antes de llegar al hotel.
I need to book my leisure vacation at the ski resort today.
Necesito reservar mis vacaciones de ocio en el hotel de estación de esquí hoy.
We want to hire a driver for the tour.
Queremos contratar un conductor para el excursión.
We want to pay with a credit card instead of cash.
Queremos pagar con tarjeta de crédito en-lugar (in lieu of) de efectivo.
Does the tour include an English-speaking guide?
¿El recorrido incluye un guía que habla inglés?

TRANSPORTATION - TRANSPORTE

Car - Auto / automóvil / coche
Bus - Autobús
Station - Estación
Train - Tren / **Train station -** Estación de tren
Train tracks - Vías del ferrocarril / **Train cart -** Carro de tren
Subway - Subterráneo
Ticket - Boleto
Taxi - Taxi
Motorcycle – Motocicleta
Scooter - Scooter
Helicopter - Helicóptero
School bus – Autobús escolar
Limousine - Limusina
Driver license - Licencia de conducir
Vehicle registration - Registro de vehículos / **License plate -** Plata de matrícula
Ticket (penalty) - Multa

Where is the public transportation?
¿Dónde está el transporte público?
Where can I buy a bus ticket?
¿Dónde puedo comprar un boleto de autobús?
Please call a taxi.
Por favor llame un taxi.
In some cities you don't need a car because you can rely on the subway.
En algunas ciudades no hace falta (there is no need) un automóvil, se cuenta con el metro.
Where is the train station?
¿Dónde está la estación de tren?
The train cart is still stuck on the tracks.
El carro del tren todavía está atascado (stuck) en las vías de ferrocarril.
The motorcycles make loud noises.
Las motocicletas hacen mucho ruido (noise).
Where can I rent a scooter?
¿Dónde puedo alquilar un scooter?
I want to schedule a helicopter tour.
Quiero programar un recorrido en helicóptero.
I want to go to the party in a limousine.
Quiero ir a la fiesta en una limusina.
Don't forget to bring your driver's license and registration.
No olvides de traer tu licencia de conducir y registro del vehículo.
The cop gave me a ticket because my license plate is expired.
La policía me dio una multa porque mi placa de matrícula estaba expirada.

Truck – Camión
Pick up truck - Camioneta
Bicycle – Bicicleta
Van - Camioneta
Gas station – Gasolinera
Gasoline - Gasolina
Tire - Llanta
Oil change – Cambio de aceite
Tire change – Cambio de llanta
Mechanic – Mecánico
Canoe - Canoa
Ship / Boat – Barco
Yacht - Yate
Sailboat - Velero / **Motorboat** – Motora
Marina - Marina
A dock - Un muelle
Cruise / cruise ship - Crucero
Ferry - Ferry
Submarine - Submarino

I have to put my bicycle in my truck.
Pongo mis bicycleta en mi camion.
Where is the gas station?
¿Donde está la gasolinera?
I need gasoline and also to put air in my tires.
Tengo que llenar gasolina y poner aire en mis llantas.
I need to take my car to the mechanic for a tire and oil change.
Necesito llevar mi automóvil al mecánico para un cambio de llantas y un cambio de aceite.
I can bring my canoe in the van.
Puedo traer mi canoa en mi camioneta.
Can I bring my yacht to the boat show at the marina?
¿Puedo llevar mi yate a la exhibición de barcos en la marina?
I prefer a motorboat instead of a sailboat.
Prefiero un bote a motor en-vez (instead) de un velero.
I want to leave my boat at the dock on the island.
Quiero dejar mi bote en el muelle de la isla.
This spot is a popular stopping point for the cruise ship.
Este lugar es un punto de parada popular para el crucero.
This was an incredible cruise.
Este era un crucero increíble.
Do you have the schedule for the ferry?
¿Tienes el horario (the schedule) para el ferry?
The submarine is yellow.
El submarino es amarillo

CITY - CIUDAD

Town / village - Pueblo
House – Casa
Home - Hogar
Apartment - Apartamento
Tower - Torre
Building - Edificio / inmueble
Skyscraper – Rascacielos
Neighborhood – Barrio
Office building – Edificio de oficinas
Location - Ubicación
Elevator – Ascensor
Stairs - Escaleras
Fence - Cerca
Construction site – Sitio de construcción
Post office – Oficina de correo
Bridge - Puente
Gate - Puerta
City hall – Alcaldía / **The mayor -** El alcalde, (f) la alcaldesa
Fire department – Departamento de bomberos

Is this a city or a village?
¿Es esta una ciudad o un pueblo?
Does he live in a house or an apartment?
¿Vive en una casa o en un apartamento?
This residential building does not have an elevator, just stairs.
El inmueble residencial no tiene ascensor, solo escaleras.
These skyscrapers are located in the new part of the city.
Estos rascacielos se encuentran (can be found) en la parte nueva de la ciudad.
The tower is tall but the building beside it is very short.
La torre es alta pero el edificio al lado es muy bajo.
This is a historical neighborhood.
Este es un barrio histórico.
There is a fence around the construction site.
Hay una cerca alrededor del sitio de construcción.
The post office is located in that office building.
La oficina de correo se encuentra en ese edificio de oficinas.
The bridge is closed today.
El puente está cerrado hoy
The gate is open.
La puerta está abierta.
The fire department is located in the building next to city hall.
El departamento de bomberos está ubicado (located) en el edificio al lado de la alcaldía.

Street - La calle
Main street - Calle principal
Parking / parking lot - Estacionamiento
Sidewalk - La acera
Traffic - Tráfico
Traffic light - Semáforo
Red light – La luz roja / **Yellow light -** La luz amarilla / **Green light –** La luz verde
Toll lane - Carril de peaje
Fast lane – Carril rápido / **Slow lane –** Carril lento
Left lane – Carril izquierdo / **Right lane –** Carril derecho
Highway – Autopista, carretera / **Intersection -** Intersección / **Tunnel –** Túnel
U-turn - Cambio de sentido / **Shortcut -** Atajo
Stop sign - Señal de stop / **Pedestrians -** Peatones / **Crosswalk -** Paso de peatones

The parking is on the main street and not on the sidewalk.
El estacionamiento está en la calle principal y no en la acera.
Where is the parking lot?
¿Dónde está el estacionamiento?
The traffic is very bad today.
El tráfico es muy malo (bad) hoy.
You must avoid the fast lane because it's a toll lane.
Debe evitar el carril rápido porque es un carril de peaje.
I hate to drive on the highway.
Odio manejar en la autopista.
At a red light you need to stop, at a yellow light you must be prepared to stop and at a green you can drive.
En una luz roja, debe detenerse, en una luz amarilla debe prepararse para detenerse, y en una luz verde puedes manejar.
I don't like traffic lights.
No me gustan los semáfaros.
At the intersection, you need to stay in the right lane instead of the left lane because that's a bus lane.
En la intersección, debe permanecer en el carril derecho en lugar del carril izquierdo porque es un carril del autobús.
The tunnel is very long, however, it seems short.
El túnel es muy largo (long), sin embargo, parece (seems) corto (short).
It's a long way.
Es un camino largo.
The next bus stop is far.
La próxima parada del autobús es lejos.
You need to turn right at the stop sign and then continue on straight.
Debe girar a la derecha en la señal de stop y luego continuar derecho.
Pedestrians use the crosswalk to cross the road.
Los peatones usan el paso de peatones para cruzar la calle.

Capital – La capital
Resort - Recurso
Port - Puerto
Road - La carretera / camino
Trail – Sendero
Bus station - Estación de autobuses
Bus stop – Parada de autobús
Night club – Club nocturno
Downtown – Centro de la ciudad
District - Distrito
County - Condado
Statue - Estatua
Monument - Monumento
Castle – Castillo
Cathedral - Catedral
Zoo – Parque zoológico
Science museum – Museo de Ciencia
Playground – Campo de recreo
Swimming pool – Piscina
Jail – Cárcel
Prison - Prisión

The capital is a major attraction point for tourists.
La capital es un importante punto de atracción para los turistas.
The resort is next to the port.
El recurso está al lado del puerto.
The night club is located in the downtown district.
El club nocturno está en el centro de la ciudad.
This statue is a monument to the city.
Esta estatua es un monumento de la ciudad.
This is an ancient castle.
Este es un castillo antiguo.
That is a beautiful cathedral.
Esta es una linda catedral.
Do you want to go to the zoo or the science museum?
¿Quieres ir al parque zoológico o al museo de ciencias?
The children are in the playground.
Los niños están en el campo de recreo.
The swimming pool is closed for the community today.
Hoy la piscina está cerrada para la comunidad.
You need to follow the trail alongside the main street to reach the bus station.
Tienes que seguir el sendero junto a la calle principal para llegar a la estación de autobuses.
There is a jail in this county, but not a prison.
Hay una cárcel en este condado, sin embargo (however), no hay el prisión.

ENTERTAINMENT - ENTRETENIMIENTO

Movie / film - Película
Theater (movie theater) - Cine
Actor - Actor
Actress - Actriz
Genre – Género
Subtitles – Subtítulos
Action - Acción
Foreign - Extranjero
Mystery – Misterio
Suspense – Suspenso
Documentary - Documentaría / **Biography** - Biografía
Drama - Drama
Comedy - Comedia
Romance - Romance
Horror – Horror
Animation - Animación
Cartoon – Dibujos animados
Director – Director / **Producer** - Productor / **Audience** – Audiencia, publico

There are three new movies at the theater that I want to see.
Hay tres nuevas películas en el cine que quiero ver.
He is a really good actor.
Él es un muy buen actor.
She is an excellent actress
Ella es una excelente actriz.
That was a good action movie
Esa fue una buena película de acción
I need subtitles when I watch a foreign film
Necesito subtítulos si veo una película extranjera.
Films of the mystery-suspense genre are usually good movies.
Las películas de género de suspenso misterioso suelen ser buenas películas.
I like documentary films. However, comedy-drama or romance films are better.
Me gustan las películas de documentarios. Aunque (although), las comedias dramáticas o románticas son superiores.
My favorite genre of movies are the horror movies.
Mi género favorito de películas es el horror.
It's fun to watch cartoons and animated movies.
Es divertido (fun) ver dibujos animados y películas animadas.
Sometimes biographies are boring to watch.
A veces las biografías son aburridas de ver.
The director and the producer can meet the audience today.
El director y el productor pueden ver a la audiencia hoy.

Entertainment - Entretenimiento
Television - Televisión (program)
Television - Televisor (actual device)
A show - Programa (as in television)
A show - Un espectáculo (as in live perfromance)
Channel – Canal
Series - Serie
Commercial - Comercial
Episode - Episodio
Anchorman - Presentador
Anchorwoman - Presentadora
News - Noticias
News station – Noticiero / estación de noticias
Screening - Proyección
Live - En vivo / en directo
Broadcast - Emisión / transmisión
Headline - Título
Viewer – Espectador
Speech – Discurso
Script - Guión
Screen - Pantalla
Camera - Cámara

It's time to buy a new television.
Es hora de comprar un nuevo televisor.
This was the first episode of this television show yet it was a long series.
Este fue el primer episodio de este programa de televisión pero era una larga seria.
There aren't any commercials on this channel.
En este canal, no hay comerciales.
This anchorman and anchorwoman work for our local news station.
Estos presentador y presentadora trabajan para nuestra estación de noticias locales.
They decided to screen a live broadcast on the news.
Decidieron proyectar una transmisión en vivo en las noticias.
The news station featured the headlines before the program began.
La estación de noticias presento los titulares antes de que comenzara el programa.
Tonight, all the details about the incident were mentioned on the news.
Esta noche, todos los detalles sobre el incidente fueron mencionados en las noticias.
The viewers wanted to hear the presidential speech today.
Los espectadores querían escuchar el discurso del presidente hoy.
I must read my script in front of the screen and the camera
Tengo que leer mi guión delante de la pantalla y la cámara.
We want to enjoy the entertainment tonight.
Queremos disfrutar del entretenimiento esta noche.

Theater (play) – Teatro
A musical - Un musical
A play - Una obra
Stage – Escenario
Audition - Audición
Performance – Actuación
Box office – Taquilla, taquillera / **Ticket –** Boleto, entrada
Singer – Cantante / **Band –** Grupo
Orchestra - Orquesta
Opera - Ópera
Music - Música
Song - Canción
Musical instrument – Instrumento musical
Drum - Tambor
Guitar - Guitarra
Piano - Piano
Trumpet – Trompeta
Violin – Violín
Flute - Flauta
Art - Arte
Gallery - Galería
Studio - Estudio
Museum – Museo

It was a great musical performance.
Fue una gran actuación musical.
Can I audition for the play on this stage?
¿Puedo hacer una audición para la obra en este escenario?
She is the lead singer of the band.
Ella es la cantante principal (main) del grupo.
I will go to the box office tomorrow to purchase tickets for the opera.
Mañana iré a la taquilla a comprar entradas para la ópera.
The orchestra needs to perform below the stage.
La orquesta necesita actuar de bajo del escenario.
I like to listen to this type of music. I hope to hear a good song.
Me gusta escuchar este tipo de música. Espero escuchar una buena canción.
The most popular musical instruments that are used in a concert are drums, guitars, pianos, trumpets, violins, and flutes.
En un concierto los instrumentos musicales más popular que se usan son tambores, guitarras, pianos, trompetas, violines, y flautas.
The art gallery has a studio for rent.
La galería de arte tiene un estudio para alquilarlo.
I went to an art museum yesterday.
Fui a un museo de arte ayer.

FOODS - COMIDAS / ALIMENTACIÓN

Grocery store - Tienda de comestibles / **Market -** Mercado
Supermarket - Supermercado
Groceries - Comestibles
Butcher shop - Carnicería / **Butcher -** Carnicero
Bakery - Panadería / **Baker -** Panadero
Breakfast – Desayunó / **Lunch –** Almuerzo / **Dinner –** Cena
Meat - Carne / **Chicken -** Pollo
Seafood – Mariscos
Milk - Leche/ **Cheese -** Queso / **Butter –** Mantequilla
Egg – Huevo / **Oil -** Aceite / **Flour -** Harina
Bread - Pan
Baked - Horneado
Cake - Pastel
Beer - Cerveza / **Wine –** Vino
Cinnamon - Canela
Powder - Polvo
Mustard - Mostaza

Where is the nearest grocery store?
¿Dónde está la más cerca tienda de comestibles?
Where can I buy meat and chicken?
¿Dónde puedo comprar carne y pollo?
I need to buy flour, eggs, milk, butter, and oil to bake my cake.
Necesito comprar harina, huevos, leche, mantequilla y aceite para hornear mi pastel.
The groceries are already in the car.
Los comestibles ya están en el auto.
It's easy to find papayas and coconuts at the supermarket.
Es fácil encontrar papayas y cocos en el supermercado.
Where can I buy beer and wine.
Donde puedo comprar cerveza y vino.
On which aisle is the cinnamon powder?
¿En qué pasillo (aisle) está el polvo de canela?
The butcher shop is near the bakery.
La carnicería esta al lado de la panadería.
I have to go to the market, to buy a half pound of meat.
Tengo que ir al mercado, para comprar media (half) libra (pound) de carne.
For lunch, we can eat seafood, and then pasta for dinner.
Para el almuerzo, podemos comer mariscos y luego pasta para la cena.
I usually eat bread with cheese for breakfast.
Normalmente como pan con queso para el desayuno.
I don't have any ketchup or mustard to put on my hotdog.
No tengo ketchup o mostaza para poner en mí salchicha.

Menu - Menú
Beef - Carne de vaca / **Lamb** - Cordero / **Pork** - Cerdo
Steak - Filete/bistec
Hamburger - Hamburguesa
Water – Agua
Salad - Ensalada
Soup - Sopa
Appetizer – Aperitivo / **Entrée** – Entrada
Cooked - Cocido
Boiled - Hervido / **Fried** - Frito / **Grilled** - A la parrilla, asado
Raw - Crudo
Coffee – Café
Dessert – Postre
Ice cream - Helado
Olive oil – Aceite de oliva
Fish – Pescado
Juice - Jugo
Tea – Té
Honey - Miel
Sugar - Azúcar

Do you have a menu in English?
¿Tiene usted un menú en inglés?
Which is preferable, the fried pork or the grilled lamb?
¿Cuál es preferible, el cerdo frito o el cordero a la parrilla?
I want to order a cup of water, a soup for my appetizer, and pizza for my entrée.
Quiero pedir un vaso de agua, una sopa para mi aperitivo, y una pizza para mi plato principal.
I want to order a steak for myself, a hamburger for my son, and ice cream for my wife.
Quiero ordenar un filete para mí, una hamburguesa para mi hijo, y un helado para mi esposa.
Which type of dessert is included with my coffee?
¿Qué tipo de postre está incluido con mi café?
Can I order a salad with a boiled egg and olive oil on the side?
¿Puedo pedir una ensalada con un huevo cocido y aceite de oliva de lado?
This fish isn't well cooked, it is still raw inside.
Este pescado, no está bien cocido, todavía está crudo.
I want to order a fruit juice instead of a soda.
Quiero ordenar un jugo de frutas en vez de una soda.
I want to order tea with a teaspoon of honey instead of sugar.
Quiero ordenar un té con una cucharadita de miel en lugar de azúcar.
The tip is 20% at this restaurant.
La propina (tip) en este restaurante es 20 por-ciento (percent).

Vegetarian - Vegetariano
Vegan – Vegano
Dairy products - Lácteos / productos de leche
Salt - Sal
Pepper - Pimienta
Flavor - Sabor
Spices - Especias
Rice - Arroz **/ Fries -** Papas fritas
Soy - Soja
Nuts - Nueces
Peanuts - Cacahuetes/ maní
Sauce - Salsa
Sandwich - Bocadillo
Mayonnaise - Mayonesa
Jelly - Mermelada
Chocolate - Chocolate **/ Cookie -** Galleta, bizcocho **/ Candy -** Dulces
Whipped cream - Crema batida
Popsicle - Paleta
Frozen - Congelado **/ Thawed –** Descongelado

I don't eat meat because I am a vegetarian.
No como carne porque soy vegetariano.
My brother won't eat dairy because he is a vegan.
Mi hermano no come lácteos porque él es un vegano.
Food tastes much better with salt, pepper, and spices.
La comida tiene mejor sabor con sal, pimienta, y especias.
The only things I have in my freezer are popsicles.
Lo único que tengo en mi congeladora son paletas heladas.
No chocolate, candy, or whipped cream until after dinner.
No chocolate, ni dulces, o crema batida hasta después de la cena.
I want to try a sample of that piece of cheese.
Quiero probar una muestra (sample) de ese trozo (slice/piece) de queso.
I have allergies to nuts and peanuts.
Tengo alergias a las nueces y al maní.
This sauce is disgusting.
Esta salsa es asquerosa.
Why do you always put mayonnaise on your sandwich?
¿Por qué siempre pones mayonesa en tu bocadillo?
The food is still frozen so we need to wait for it to thaw.
La comida todavía está congelada, por eso debemos esperar a que se descongele.
Please bring me a bowl of cereal and a slice of toasted bread with jelly.
Por favor dame un tazón de cereal y una rebanada de pan tostado con mermelada.
It's healthier to eat rice instead of fries.
Es más saludable comer arroz que papas fritas.

VEGETABLES - VERDURAS / VEGETALES

Grilled vegetables – Vegetales asados / **Steamed vegetables** – Verduras al vapor
Tomato - Tomate
Carrot - Zanahoria
Lettuce - Lechuga
Radish - Rábano
Beet - Remolacha
Eggplant - Berenjena
Bell Pepper – Pimiento / **Hot pepper** – Ají picante
Celery - Apio
Spinach - Espinacas
Cabbage - Col / **Cauliflower** - Coliflor
Beans – Frijoles
Corn - Maíz
Garlic - Ajo / **Onion** - Cebolla
Artichoke - Alcachofa

Grilled vegetables or steamed vegetables are popular side dishes at restaurants.
Las verduras a la parrilla o las verduras al vapor son platos populares en los restaurantes.
I put carrots, bell peppers, lettuce, and radishes in my salad.
Yo pongo zanahorias, pimientos, lechuga, y rábanos en mi ensalada.
It's not hard to grow tomatoes.
No es difícil cultivar tomates.
Eggplant can be cooked or fried.
La berenjena se puede cocinar o freír.
I like to put beets in my salad.
Me gusta poner remolachas en la ensalada.
Why are chili peppers so spicy?
¿Por qué estos chili pimientos son tan picantes?
Celery and spinach have natural vitamins.
El apio y la espinaca tienen vitaminas naturales.
Fried cauliflower tastes better than fried cabbage.
Coliflor frito es más agradable que col frito.
Rice and beans are my favorite side dish.
El arroz y los frijoles son mi plato favorito
I like to put butter on corn
Me gusta poner mantequilla al maíz.
Garlic is an important ingredient in many cuisines.
El ajo es un ingrediente importante en muchas cocinas.
Where is the onion powder?
¿Dónde está el polvo de cebolla?
Artichokes are difficult to peel.
Las alcachofas son difíciles de pelar.

Cucumber – Pepino
Lentil - Lenteja
Peas - Guisante / chícharos
Green onion – Cebolla verde
Herbs - Hierbas
Parsley - Perejil **/ Cilantro -** Cilantro
Basil - Albahaca **/ Dill -** Eneldo
Mint - Yerba buena
Potatoes – Papas / patatas **/ Sweet Potato -** Batata
Mushroom – Hongo
Asparagus - Espárragos
Seaweed – Algas marinas
Pumpkin – Calabaza **/ Squash -** Calabaza **/ Zucchini -** Calabacín
Chick peas – Garbanzos
Vegetable garden – Huerto / jardín de vegetales

I want to order lentil soup.
Quiero ordenar sopa de lentejas.
Please put the green onion in the refrigerator.
Por favor ponga las cebollitas verdes en el refrigerador.
The most common kitchen herbs are basil, cilantro, dill, parsley, and mint.
Las hierbas más comunes en la cocina son la albahaca, el cilantro, el eneldo, el perejil, y la yerba buena.
Some of the most common vegetables for tempura are sweet potatoes and mushrooms.
Algunas verduras de las más comunes para tempura son las batatas y los hongos.
I want to order vegetarian sushi with asparagus and cucumber, along with a side of seaweed salad.
Quiero pedir sushi vegetariano con espárragos y pepino y una adición de ensalada de algas.
I enjoy eating pumpkin seeds as a snack.
Disfruto comer semillas (seeds) de calabaza como merienda.
I need to water my vegetable garden.
Necesito regar mi huerto.
The potatoes in the field are ready to harvest.
Las papas en el campo (field) están listas para cosecharlas.
Chickpeas are the main ingredient to make hummus.
Los garbanzos son el ingrediente principal para hacer humus.
Zucchini and squash are from the same family of vegetables.
El calabacín y la calabaza son de la misma familia de verduras.
Pickled ginger is extremely healthy for you.
El jengibre en escabeche es extremadamente saludable (healthy) para ti.
The tomatoes are fresh but the cucumbers are rotten.
Los tomates son frescos (fresh) pero los pepinos están podridos (rotten).

FRUITS - FRUTAS

Apple - Manzana / **Banana -** Banana / **Peach -** Durazno
Orange - Naranja / **Grapefruit -** Toronja
Tropical fruit - Fruta tropical
Papaya - Papaya
Coconut - Coco
Cherry - Cereza
Raisin - Pasa / **Prune -** Ciruela la seca
Dates - Dátiles
Fig - Higo
Fruit salad - Ensalada de frutas
Dried fruit - Fruta seca
Apricot - Albaricoque
Pear - Pera
Avocado - Aguacate
Ripe - Maduro

Can I add raisins to the apple pie?
¿Puedo agregar pasas a la tarta (pie) de manzana?
Orange juice is a wonderful source of Vitamin C.
El jugo de naranja es una maravillosa fuente (source) de vitamina C.
Grapefruits are extremely beneficial for your health.
Las toronjas son extremadamente beneficiosas para su salud (health).
I have a peach tree in my front yard.
Tengo un árbol de durazno en mi jardin.
It's easy to find papayas and coconuts at the supermarket.
Es fácil encontrar papayas y cocos en el supermercado.
I want to travel to Japan to see the famous cherry blossom.
Quiero viajar al Japón para ver la famosa flor de cerezas.
Bananas are tropical fruits.
Las bananas son frutas tropicales.
I want to mix dates and figs in my fruit salad.
Quiero mezclar dátiles e higos en mi ensalada de frutas.
Apricots and prunes are my favorite dried fruits.
Los albaricoques y las ciruelas son mis frutas secas (dried) favoritas.
Pears are delicious.
Las peras son deliciosas.
The avocados aren't ripe yet.
Los aguacates aún no están maduros (ripe).
The green apple is very sour.
La manzana verde es muy agria (sour).
The unripe peach is usually bitter.
El durazno inmaduro (unripe) suele (usually) ser amargo (bitter).

Fruit tree - Árbol de frutas
Citrus - Cítricos
Lemon - Limón
Lime - Lima
Pineapple - Piña
Melon - Melón
Watermelon - Sandía
Strawberry - Fresa
Berry - Baya / moras
Raspberry - Frambuesa
Blueberry - Arándano
Grape - Uva
Pomegranate - Granada
Plum - Ciruela
Olive - Aceituna
Grove - Arboleda

Strawberries grow during the Spring.
Las fresas crecen durante la primavera.
How much does the watermelon juice cost?
¿Cuánto cuesta el jugo de sandía?
I have a pineapple plant inside a pot.
Tengo una planta de piña en una maceta (plant pot).
Melons grow on the ground.
Los melones crecen en la tierra (ground).
I am going to the fruit-tree section of the nursery today to purchase a few citrus trees.
Hoy voy a la sección de árboles frutales del vivero (nursery) para comprar algunos cítricos.
There are many raspberries on the bush.
Hay muchas frambuesas en el arbusto (bush).
Blueberry juice is very sweet.
El jugo de arándano es muy dulce.
Berriess are acidic fruits.
Las bayas son frutas ácidas.
Pomegranate juice contains a very high level of antioxidants.
El jugo de la granada contiene un nivel (level) muy alto de antioxidantes.
I need to pick the grapes to make the wine.
Necesito recoger las uvas para hacer el vino.
Plums are seasonal fruits.
Las ciruelas son frutas temporadas (seasonal).
I must add either lemon juice or lime juice to my salad
Debo agregar jugo de limón o jugo de lima en mi ensalada.
I have an olive grove in my backyard.
Tengo un olivar en mí jardín.

SHOPPING - COMPRAS

Clothes - Ropa
Clothing store - Tienda de ropa
For sale - Se vende / en venta
Hat - Sombrero
Shirt - Camisa
Shoes - Zapatos
Skirt - Falda / **Dress -** Vestido
Pants - Pantalones / **Shorts -** Pantalones cortos
Suit - Traje / **Vest -** Chaleco / **Tie -** Corbata
Uniform - Uniforme
Belt - Cinturón
Socks - Calcetines
Gloves - Guantes
Glasses - Lentes / **Sunglasses -** Gafas
Size - Talla / tamaño
Small - Pequeño, **(f)** pequeña
Medium - Medio
Large - Grande
Thin - Delgado, **(f)** delgada / **Thick -** Grueso, **(f)** gruesa
Thrift store - Tienda de segunda mano

There are a lot of clothes for sale today.
Hoy hay mucha ropa que se vende.
Does this hat look good?
¿Se ve bien este sombrero?
I am happy with this shirt and these shoes.
Estoy contento con esta camisa y estos zapatos.
She prefers a skirt instead of a dress.
Ella prefiere una falda en vez de un vestido.
These pants aren't my size.
Estos pantalones no son de mi talla.
Where can I find a thrift store? I want to buy a suit, a vest, and a tie.
¿Dónde puedo encontrar una tienda de segunda mano? Quiero comprar un traje, un chaleco, y una corbata.
There are uniforms for school at the clothing store.
Hay uniformes para la escuela en la tienda de ropa.
I forgot my socks, belt, and shorts at your house.
Olvidé mis calcetines, cinturón y pantalones cortos en tu casa.
These gloves are a size too small. Do you have a medium size?
Estos guantes son de una talla demasiado pequeña. ¿Tienes una talla mediana?
Today I don't need my reading glasses. I only need my sunglasses.
No necesito mis lentes para leer hoy. Solo necesito mis gafas.

Jacket - Chaqueta
Scarf - Bufanda
Mittens - Guantes
Sleeve - Mangas
Boots (rain, winter) - Botas
Sweater - Suéter
Bathing suit - Traje de baño/bañador
Flip flops - Chanclas / chancletas
Tank top - Camiseta
Sandals - Sandalias
Heels - Tacones
On sale - En venta
Expensive - Costoso / caro
Free - Gratis
Discount - Descuento
Cheap - Barato
Shopping - Compras
Mall - Centro comercial

We are going to the mountain today so don't forget your jacket, mittens, and scarf.
Hoy vamos a la montaña que no te olvides tu chaqueta, los guantes y la bufanda.
I have long sleeve shirts and short sleeve shirts.
Tengo camisas de mangas largas y de mangas cortas.
Boots and sweaters are meant for winter.
Botas y suéter se usan en el invierno (winter).
At the beach, I wear a bathing suit and flip flops.
En la playa (beach) voy con un bañador y chanclas.
I want to buy a tank top for summer.
Quiero comprar una camiseta para el verano (summer).
I can't wear heels on the beach, only sandals.
No puedo usar tacones en la playa, solo sandalias.
What's on sale today?
¿Qué está en venta hoy?
This is free.
Esto es gratis.
Even though this cologne and this perfume are discounted, they are still very expensive.
A pesar de que este colone y este perfume tienen descuentos, todavía estan muy caros.
These items are very cheap.
Estos artículos son muy baratos.
I can go shopping only on weekends.
Puedo ir de compras solamente en fin-de-semanas (weekend).
Is the local mall far?
¿Está lejos el centro comercial local?

Business hours - Horas de trabajo
Store - Tienda
Business hours - Horas de trabajo / horario de trabajo
Open - Abierto / **Closed -** Cerrado
Entrance - Entrada / **Exit -** Salida
Shopping cart - Carrito de compras
Shopping basket - Cesta de compras
Shopping bag - Bolsa de la compra
Toy store - Tienda de juguetes / **Toy -** Juguete
Book store - Librería
Music store - Tienda de música
Jeweler - Joyero / **Jewelry -** Joyería / **Gold -** Oro / **Silver -** Plata
Necklace - Collar / **Bracelet -** Pulsera / **Earrings -** Pendientes / **Diamond -** Diamante
Gift - Regalo
Coin - Moneda
Antique - Antiguo / **Dealer -** Comerciante

What are your business hours?
¿Cuál es su horario de trabajo?
What time does the store open?
¿A qué hora abre la tienda?
What time does the store close?
¿A qué hora se cierra la tienda?
Where is the entrance?
¿Donde está la entrada?
Where is the exit?
¿Donde está la salida?
My children want to go to the toy store so that they can fill up the shopping cart with toys.
Mis hijos quieren ir a la juguetera para rellenar el carrito con muchos juguetes.
I need a large shopping basket when I go to the supermarket.
Necesito una gran cesta de compras cuando voy al supermercado.
Bookstores are almost non-existent since today everything that's for sale is online.
Las librerías casi no existen ya que hoy todo lo que está en venta, se vende por online.
It's difficult to find a music store these days.
Es difícil encontrar una tienda de música en estos días.
The jeweler sells gold and silver.
El joyero vende oro y plata.
I want to buy a diamond necklace.
Quiero comprar un collar de diamantes.
This bracelet and those pair of earrings are gifts for my daughter.
Esta pulsera y esos pendientes son regalos para mi hija.
He is an antique coin dealer.
Él es un comerciante de monedas antiguas.

FAMILY - FAMILIA

Mother - Madre
Father - Padre
Son - Hijo
Daughter - Hija
Brother - Hermano
Sister - Hermana
Husband - Marido / esposo
Wife - Esposa / mujer
Parents - Padres
Child - Niño / niña
Baby - Bebé
Grandparents - Abuelos
Grandfather - Abuelo
Grandmother - Abuela
Grandson - Nieto
Granddaughter - Nieta
Grandchildren - Nietos
Nephew - Sobrino **/ Niece -** Sobrina
Cousin - Primo /prima

I have a big family.
Tengo una gran familia.
My brother and sister are here.
Mi hermano y mi hermana están aquí.
The mother and father want to spend time with their child.
La madre y el padre quieren pasar-tiempo (to spend time) con su hijo.
He wants to bring his son and daughter.
Quiere traer a su hijo e hija.
The grandfather wants to take his grandson to the movie.
El abuelo quiere llevar a su nieto al cine.
The grandmother needs to give her granddaughter money.
La abuela necesita dar dinero (money) a su nieta.
The grandparents want to spend time with their grandchildren.
Los abuelos quieren pasar el tiempo con sus nietos.
The husband and wife have a new baby.
El esposo y la esposa tienen un nuevo bebé.
I want to go to the park with my niece and nephew.
Quiero ir al parque (park) con mi sobrina y sobrino.
My cousin wants to see his children.
Mi primo quiere ver a sus hijos.
That man is a good parent.
Ese hombre es un buen padre.

Aunt - Tía / **Uncle** - Tío
Man - Hombre / **Woman** - Mujer
Stepfather - Padrastro / **Stepmother** - Madrastra
Stepbrother - Hermanastro / **Stepsister** - Hermanastra
Stepson - Hijastro / **Stepdaughter** - Hijastra
Half brother - Medio hermano / **Half sister** - Media hermana
In laws - Suegros
Ancestor - Antepasado / **Family tree** - Árbol genealógico
Generation - Generación
First born - Primogénito / **Only child** - Hijo único
Relatives - Parientes / **Family members** - Familares, miembros de la familia
Twins - Gemelos
Pregnant - Embarazada
Adult - Adulto
Neighbor - Vecino, vecina / **Friend** - Amigo, amiga / **Roomate** - Compañero de cuarto
Adopted child - Niño adoptado
Orphan - Huérfano

My aunt and uncle are here for a visit.
Mi tía y mi tío me visitan.
He is their only child.
Él es su hijo único.
My wife is pregnant with twins.
Mi esposa está embarazada y son gemelos.
He is their eldest son.
Él es el primogénito.
The first-born child usually takes on all the responsibilities.
El primogénito generalmente asume todas las responsabilidades.
I was able to find all my relatives and ancestors on my family tree.
En mi árbol genealógico encontré a mis parientes y mis antepasados.
My parents' generation loved disco music.
La generación de mis padres amaban la música disco.
Their adopted child was an orphan
Él hijo adoptivo era un huérfano.
I like my in-laws.
Me gustan mis suegros.
I have a nice neighbor.
Tengo un buen vecino
We need to choose a godfather for his daughter.
Necesitamos elegir un padrino para su hija.
She considers her stepson as her real son.
Ella considera a su hijastro como su verdadero hijo.
She is his stepdaughter.
Ella es su hijastra.

HUMAN BODY - CUERPO HUMANO

Head - Cabeza
Face - Cara
Eye - Ojo / **Nose** - Nariz
Ear - Oreja
Mouth - Boca / **Lips** - Labios
Tongue - Lengua
Cheek - Mejilla
Chin - Mentón
Neck - Cuello / **Throat** - Garganta
Forehead - Frente / **Eyebrow** - Ceja / **Eyelashes** - Pestañas
Hair - Cabello / pelo
Beard - Barba / **Mustache** - Bigotes
Tooth - Diente

My chin, cheeks, mouth, lips, and eyes are all part of my face.
Mi mentón, mejillas, boca, labios y ojos son parte de mi cara.
He has small ears.
Él tiene orejas pequeñas.
I have a cold so my nose, eyes, mouth, and tongue are affected.
Tengo un resfriado que afectan mi nariz, ojos, boca y lengua.
The five senses are sight, touch, taste, smell, and hearing.
La vista, el tacto, el gusto, el olfato y el oído son los cinco sentidos.
I am washing my face right now.
Me estoy lavando la cara ahora mismo.
I have a headache
Tengo un dolor de cabeza.
My eyebrows are too long.
Mis cejas son demasiado largas.
He must shave his beard and mustache.
Debe afeitarse la barba y los bigotes.
I want to brush my teeth in the morning.
Quiero cepillar los dientes por la mañana.
She puts a lot of makeup on her cheeks and a lot of lipstick on her lips.
Tiene mucho maquillaje en sus mejillas y mucho pinte de labios.
Her hair covered her forehead.
Su cabello cubría su frente.
My hair is very long.
Mi pelo es muy largo.
She has a long neck.
Ella tiene un cuello largo.
I have a sore throat.
Tengo un dolor de garganta.

Shoulder - Hombro
Chest - Pecho
Arm - Brazo / **Elbow -** Codo / **Wrist -** Muñeca
Hand - Mano / **Palm** (of hand) - Palma
Finger - Dedo
Thumb - Pulgar
Back - Espalda
Brain - Cerebro / **Lungs -** Pulmones / **Heart -** Corazón / **Kidneys -** Riñones
Liver - Hígado / **Stomach -** Estómago / **Intestines -** Intestinos
Leg - Pierna / **Ankle -** Tobillo
Foot - Pie
Toe - Dedo del pie
Nail - Uña
Joint - Articulación
Muscle - Músculo
Skeleton - Esqueleto / **Bone -** Hueso
Spine - Columna vertebral / **Ribs -** Costillas / **Skull -** Cráneo
Skin -Piel
Vein - Vena

In the human body, the chest is located below the shoulders
En el cuerpo humano, el pecho está debajo de los hombros.
He has a problem with his stomach.
Él tiene un problema con su estómago.
I need to strengthen my arms and legs.
Necesito fortalecer mis brazos y piernas.
I accidentally hit his wrist with my elbow.
Accidentalmente golpeé su muñeca con mi codo.
I have pain in every part of my body especially in my hand, ankle, and back.
Me duelen todas las partes de mi cuerpo, especialmente mi mano, tobillo y espalda.
I want to cut my fingernails and my toenails
Tengo que cortarme las uñas de las manos y los pies.
I need a new bandage for my thumb.
Necesito un vendaje nuevo para mi pulgar.
I have muscle and joint pains.
Tengo dolor de los músculos y las articulaciones.
You should change the cast on your foot at least once a month.
Debes cambiar el yeso (cast) en tu pie por los menos una vez al mes.
The spine is an important part of the skeleton.
La columna vertebral es la parte importante del esqueleto.
I have beautiful skin.
Tengo una piel bonita.
The brain, heart, kidney, lungs, and liver are internal organs.
El cerebro, el corazón, los riñones, los pulmones y el hígado son órganos internos.

HEALTH AND MEDICAL - SALUD Y MÉDICO

Disease - Enfermedad
Bacteria - Bacteria
Sick - Enfermo
Clinic - Clínica
Headache - Dolor de cabeza
Earache - Dolor de oídos
Pharmacy - Farmacia / **Prescription** - Prescripción
Symptoms - Síntomas
Nausea - Náusea / **Stomachache** - Dolor de estómago
Allergy - Alergia
Antibiotic - Antibiótico / **Penicillin** - Penicilina
Sore throat - Dolor de garganta / **Fever** - Fiebre / **Flu** - Gripe
To cough - Toser / **A cough** - Tos
Infection - Infección
Injury - Lesión / **Scar** - Cicatriz
Ache / pain - Dolor
Intensive care - Cuidados intensivos
Bandage - Vendaje

Are you in good health?
¿Estás en buena salud?
These bacteria caused this disease.
Estas bacterias causaron esta enfermedad.
He is very sick.
Él está muy enfermo.
I have a bad headache today so I must go to the pharmacy to refill my prescription.
Hoy me duele mucho la cabeza, así que debo ir a la farmacia para rellenar mi receta.
The main symptoms of food poisoning are nausea and stomach ache.
Los síntomas principales de intoxicación alimentaria son náuseas y dolor de estómago.
I have an allergy to penicillin, so I need another antibiotic.
Soy alérgico a la penicilina, por eso necesito otro antibiótico.
What do I need to treat an earache?
¿Qué necesito para tratar un dolor de oído?
I need to go to the clinic for my fever and sore throat.
Necesito ir a la clínica por la fiebre y dolor de garganta.
The bandage won't help your infection.
El vendaje no ayudará tu infección.
I have a serious injury so I must go to intensive care.
Tengo una lesión muy grave, así que debo ir al centro de cuidados intensivos.
I have muscle and joint pains today.
Hoy tengo dolor de los músculos y las articulaciones.

Hospital - Hospital
Doctor - Doctor
Nurse - Enfermera
Family Doctor - Médico de familia / **Pediatrician -** Pediatra
Medicine / medication - Medicina / medicación, **Pills -** Pastillas / píldoras
Heartburn - Acidez
Paramedic - Paramédico
Emergency room - Sala de emergencias
Health insurance - Seguro de salud / seguro médical
Patient - Paciente
Surgery - Cirugía / **Surgeon -** Cirujano
Anesthesia - Anestesia
Local anesthesia - Anestesia local / **General anesthesia -** Anestesia general
Wheelchair - Silla de ruedas / **A walker -** Un caminante / **A cane -** Un bastón
Stretcher - Camilla
Dialysis - Diálisis / **Insulin -** Insulina
Temperature - Temperatura / **Thermometer -** Termómetro
A shot - Inyección / **Needle -** Aguja / **Syringe -** Jeringuilla

Where is the closest hospital?
¿Dónde está el hospital más cercano?
I am seeing the nurse now before the doctor.
Estoy viendo a la enfermera ahora antes del doctor.
The paramedics can take her to the emergency room but she doesn't have health insurance.
Los paramédicos pueden llevarla a la sala de emergencias, pero no tiene seguro médical.
The doctor told the patient to go home.
El doctor dijo al paciente que se vaya a su casa.
He needs knee surgery.
Necesita cirugía de la rodilla (knee).
The surgeon requires general anesthesia in order to operate.
El cirujano requiere anestesia general para poder operar.
Does the patient need a wheelchair or a stretcher?
¿El paciente necesita una silla de ruedas o una camilla?
I have to take medicine every day.
Tengo que tomar medicamentos todos los días.
Do you have any pills for heartburn?
¿Tienes alguna píldora para la acidez estomacal?
Where is the closest dialysis center?
¿Dónde está el centro de diálisis más cercano?
Where can I buy insulin for my diabetes?
¿Dónde puedo comprar insulina para mi diabetes?
I need a thermometer to take my temperature.
Necesito un termómetro para tomarme la temperatura.

Stroke - Derrame cerebral
Blood - Sangre / **Blood pressure** - Presión sanguínea
Heart attack - Ataque de corazón
Cancer - Cáncer / **Chemotherapy** - Quimioterapia
To help - Ayudar
Germs - Gérmenes / **Virus** - Virus
Vaccine - Vacuna / **A cure** - Una cura / **To cure** - Curar
Cholesterol - Colesterol / **Nutrition** - Nutrición / **Diet** - Dieta
Blind - Ciego / **Deaf** - Sordo / **Mute** - Mudo
Nursing home - Asilo de ancianos
Disability - Invalidez / **Handicap** - Desventaja / **Paralysis** - Parálisis
Depression - Depresión / **Anxiety** - Ansiedad
Dentist - Dentista
X-ray - Radiografía
Cavity - Cavidad
Tooth paste - Pasta dental / **Tooth brush** - Cepillo de dientes
Fat (person) - Gordo, **(f)** gorda / **The fat** - La grasa
Skinny - Flaco, **(f)** flaca / **Thin** - Delgado, **(f)** delgada
Young - Joven / **Elderly** - Anciano

A stroke is caused by a lack of blood flow to the brain.
Un derrame cerebral es causado por la falta de flujo sanguíneo en el cerebro.
These are the symptoms of a heart attack.
Estos son los síntomas de un ataque de corazón.
Chemotherapy is used to treat cancer.
La quimioterapia se usa para tratar el cáncer.
Proper nutrition is very important and you must avoid foods that are high in cholesterol.
Una adecuada nutrición es muy importante y debe evitar los alimentos con alto contenido de colesterol.
I need to go on a diet.
Necesito ponerme en dieta.
There is no cure for this virus, only a vaccine.
No hay cura para este virus, solamente una vacuna.
The nursing home is open 365 days a year.
El hogar de ancianos está abierto los 365 días del año.
I don't like suffering from depression and anxiety.
No me place sufrir de depresión y ansiedad.
Soap and water kill germs.
El jabón y el agua matan los gérmenes.
The dentist took X-rays of my teeth to check for cavities.
En el dentista toma radiografías para revisar las cavidades en los dientes.
My toothpaste has the same colors as my toothbrush.
Mi pasta dentífrica tiene los mismos colores que mi cepillo.

EMERGENCY & DISASTERS - EMERGENCIA Y DESASTRES

Help - Ayuda
Fire - Incendio
Ambulance - Ambulancia
First aid - Auxilios primeros
CPR - RCP
Emergency number - Número de emergencia
Accident - Accidente
A car accident - Un accidente automovilístico
Death - Muerte / **Deadly** - Mortal / **Fatal** - Fatal
Lightly wounded - Levemente herido
Moderately wounded - Moderadamente herido
Seriously wounded - Gravemente herido
Fire truck - Camión de bomberos / **Siren** - Sirena
Fire extinguisher - Extintor
Police - Policía / **Police station** - Estación de policía
Robbery - Robo
Thief - Ladrón

There is a fire. I need to call for help.
Hay un incendio. Necesito ayuda.
I need to call an ambulance.
Tengo que llamar a una ambulancia.
That accident was bad.
Ese accidente fue malo.
The thief wants to steal my money.
El ladrón quiere robar mi dinero.
The car crash was fatal. In addition, to the two deaths, four others suffered serious injuries, one was moderately wounded, and two were lightly wounded.
El accidente automovilístico fue fatal. Además de las dos muertes, otros cuatros sufrieron graves heridas, una fue moderadamente y dos resultaron levemente heridas.
To know how to perform CPR is a very important first-aid knowledge.
Saber cómo realizar la RCP es un conocimiento muy importante de auxilios primeros.
What's the emergency number in this country?
¿Cuál es el número de emergencia en este país?
The police are on their way.
La policía está en camino.
I must call the police station to report a robbery.
Tengo que llamar la policía para denunciar un robo.
The siren of the fire truck is very loud.
La sirena del camión de bomberos es muy ruidosa.
Where is the fire extinguisher?
¿Dónde está el extintor de incendios?

Fire hydrant - La boca de incendio
Fireman - Bombero
Emergency situation - Situación de emergencia
Explosion - Explosión
Rescue - Rescate
Natural disaster - Desastre natural
Destruction - Destrucción / **Damage -** Daño
Hurricane - Huracán
Tornado - Tornado
Hurricane shelter - Refugio contra huracanes
Flood - Inundio
Storm - Tormenta
Snowstorm - Nevada / tormenta de nieve
Hail - Granizo
Refuge - Refugio
Caused - Causó
Safety - La seguridad
Drought - Sequía
Famine - Hambruna
Poverty - Pobreza
Epidemic - Epidemia / **Pandemic -** Pandemia

It's prohibited to park by the fire hydrant in case of a fire.
Es prohibido estacionarse al lado de una boca de incendio, en caso de un incendio.
When there is a fire, the first to arrive on scene are the firemen.
En un incendio los primeros a llegar son los bomberos.
There is a fire. I need to call for help.
Hay un incendio. Necesito ayuda.
In an emergency situation everyone needs to be rescued.
En una situación de emergencia cada uno necesita rescatarse.
The gas explosion led to a natural disaster.
La explosión del gas causo a un desastre natural.
We used the hurricane shelter as refuge.
Utilizamos el refugio debido al huracán.
The hurricane caused a lot of destruction and damage in its path.
El huracán causó mucha destrucción y daño a su paso.
The tornado destroyed the town.
El tornado destruyó la ciudad.
The drought led to famine and a lot of poverty.
La sequía provocó hambre y mucha pobreza.
There were three days of floods following the storm.
Hubo tres días de inundaciones después de la tormenta.
This is a snowstorm and not a hail storm.
Esta es una tormenta de nieve y no de granizo.

Dangerous - Peligroso
Danger - Peligro
Warning - Advertencia
Earthquake - Terremoto
Disaster - Desastre
Disaster area - Área de desastre
Evacuation - Evacuación
Mandatory - Obligatorio
Safe place - Lugar seguro
Blackout - Apagón
Rainstorm - Tormenta de lluvia
Lightning - Rayo / relámpago
Thunder - Trueno
Avalanche - Avalancha
Heatwave - Ola de calor
Rip current - Corriente de resaca
Tsunami - Tsunami
Whirlpool - Remolino

We need to stay in a safe place during the earthquake.
Necesitamos permanecer en un lugar seguro durante el terremoto.
Heatwaves are usually in the summer.
Las olas de calor suelen ser en el verano.
This is a disaster area, therefore there is a mandatory evacuation order.
En la área del desastre, la evacuación es mandatoria.
There was a blackout for three hours due to the rainstorm.
Tuvimos un apagón durante tres horas debido a la tormenta.
Be careful during the snowstorm since there might be the risk of an avalanche.
Ten cuidado durante la nevada porque puede existir el riesgo de avalancha.
There is a tsunami warning today.
Hoy hay una alerta de tsunami.
You can't swim against a rip current.
No puedes nadar contra una corriente de resaca.
There is a deadly whirlpool in the ocean.
Hay un remolino mortal en el océano.

HOME - CASA / HOGAR

House - Casa
Living room - Sala
Couch - Diván
Sofa - Sofá
Door - Puerta
Closet - Armario
Stairway - Escalera
Rug - Alfombra
Curtain - Cortina
Window - Ventana
Floor - Suelo
Floor (as in level) - Nivel / piso
Fireplace / Chimney - Chimenea
Candle - Vela
Laundry detergent - Detergente
Laundry - Lavandería

He has a fireplace at his home.
El tiene una chimenea en su casa.
The living room is missing a couch and a sofa.
Al salón le faltan un diván y un sofá.
I must buy a new door for my closet.
Debo comprar una nueva puerta para mi armario.
The spiral staircase is beautiful.
La escalera de caracol es hermosa.
There aren't any curtains on the windows.
No hay cortinas en las ventanas.
I have a marble floor on the first floor and a wooden floor on the second floor.
Tengo un suelo de mármol en el primer piso y uno de madera en el segundo.
I can only light this candle now.
Ahora puedo solo encender esta vela.
I can clean the floors today and then I want to arrange the closet.
Hoy puedo limpiar los pisos y luego quiero arreglar el armario.
I need to wash the rug today with laundry detergent and then hang it to dry.
Necesito lavar la alfombra hoy con detergente para ropa y luego colgarla para que se seque.

Silverware - El cubierto
Knife - El cuchillo
Fork - El tenedor
Spoon - La cuchara
Teaspoon - La cucharita
Kitchen - Cocina
A cup - Una taza
Plate - Plato
Bowl - Tazón
Napkin - Servilleta
Table - La mesa
Placemat - Mantel individual
Table cloth - Un mantel
Glass (material) **-** Vidrio
A glass (cup) **-** Un vaso
Oven - Horno
Stove - Estufa
Pot (cooking) **-** Olla
Pan - Sartén
Shelve - Estantería
Cabinet - Gabinete
Pantry - Despensa
Drawer - Cajón

The knives, spoons, teaspoons, and forks are inside the drawer in the kitchen.
Los cuchillos, cucharas, cucharaditas y tenedores están dentro del cajón de la cocina.
There aren't enough cups, plates, and silverware on the table for everyone.
No hay suficientes tazas, platos y cubiertos en la mesa para todos.
The napkins are underneath the bowls.
Las servilletas están debajo de los tazones.
I need to set the placemats on top of the table cloth.
Necesito colocar los manteles individuales sobre el mantel.
There is canned food in the pantry.
Hay comida enlatada (canned) en la despensa.
Where are the toothpicks?
¿Dónde están los palillos de dientes?
Can I use wine glasses on the shelf for the champagne?
¿Puedo utilizar copas de vino en el estante para el champán?
The pizza is in the oven.
La pizza esta en el horno.
The pots and pans are in the cabinet.
Las ollas y las sartenes están en el gabinete.
The stove is broken.
La estufa está rota (broken).

Bedroom - Dormitorio
Bed - Cama
Blanket - Manta
Bed sheet - Sábana
Mattress - Colchón
Pillow - Almohada
Mirror - Espejo
Chair - Silla
Dinning room - Comedor
Hallway - Pasillo
Towel - Toalla
Bathtub - Bañera
Shower - Ducha
Sink - Lavabo
Soap - Jabón
Bathroom - Baño
Bag - Bolso / **Box -** Caja
Keys - Llaves

The master bedroom is at the end of the hallway, and the dining room is downstairs.
El dormitorio principal está al final del pasillo y el comedor está abajo.
The mirror looks good in the bedroom.
El espejo se ve bien en el dormitorio.
I have to buy a new bed and a new mattress.
Tengo que comprar una cama nueva y un colchón nuevo.
Where are the blankets and bed sheets?
¿Dónde están las mantas y las sábanas?
My pillows are on the chair.
Mis almohadas están encima (on top) de la silla.
These towels are for drying your hand.
Estas toallas son para secarse sus manos.
The bathtub, shower, and the sink are new.
La bañera, la ducha y el lavabo son nuevos.
I need soap to wash my hands
Necesito jabón para lavar mis manos
The guest bathroom is in the corner of the hallway.
El baño de huéspedes (guests) está en la esquina (corner) del pasillo.
How many boxes does he have?
¿Cuántas cajas tiene él?
I want to put my items in the plastic bag.
Quiero poner mis artículos en la bolsa de plástico.
I need to bring my keys with me.
Necesito traer mis llaves conmigo.

Room - Habitación
Balcony - Balcón
Roof - Techo
Ceiling - Techo
Wall - Pared
Carpet - Tapete
Attic - Ático
Basement - Sótano
Trash - Basura
Garbage can - Contenido de basura
Driveway - Entrada de autos
Garden / backyard - Jardín
Doormat - Felpudo
Jar - Frasco / tarro

I can install new windows for my balcony.
Puedo instalar nuevas ventanas para mi balcón.
I must install a new roof.
Voy a instalar un nuevo techo.
The color of my ceiling is white.
El color de mi techo es blanco.
I must paint the walls.
Tengo que pintar las paredes.
The attic is an extra room in the house.
El ático es una habitación adicional de la casa.
The kids are playing either in the basement or the backyard.
Los niños juegan en el sótano o en el jardín.
All the glass jars are outside on the doormat.
Todos los frascos de vidrio están afuera sobre el felpudo.
The garbage can is blocking the driveway.
El bote de basura está bloqueando el camino de entrada.

Basic Grammatical Requirements of the Spanish Language

Present Tense Indicative: Regular Verbs

In the Spanish language all infinitive forms of the verbs end in: "ar", "er", "ir".

The verbs are conjugated in the present tense of the indicative form by just adding the following personal endings to the stem of the verb.

	Hablar	Comer	Vivir
Yo	hablo	como	vivo
Tu	hablas	comes	vives
El, ella, usted	habla	come	vive
Nostro/as	hablamos	comemos	vivemos
Vosotros/as	hablais	comeis	vivis
Ellos, ellas, ustedes	hablan	comen	viven
AR VERBS	**ER VERBS**	**IR VERBS**

The asterick represents irregular verbs.

AR VERBS	ER VERBS	IR VERBS
Comprar - To buy	**Beber** - To drink	**Abrir** - To open
Bailar - To dance	**Comer** - To eat	**Escribir** - To write
Cambiar - To change	**To leer** - To read	**Assistir** - To assist
Desear - To wish	**Creer** - To believe	**Insistir** - To insist
Preguntar - To ask	**Responder** - To respond	**Recibir** - To receive
Trabajar - To work	**Vender** - To sell	***Preferir** - To prefer
Necesitar - To need	**Leer** - To read	***Incluir** - To include
Tomar - To take	***Querer** - To want	***Salir** - To leave
Llegar - To arrive	**Obedecer** - To obey	***Servir** - To serve
Ayudar - To help	***Tener** - To have	***Decir** - To say
Estudiar - To study	**Comprender** - To understand	***Sentir** - To feel
Escuchar - To hear	***Saber** - To know	
Viajar - To travel		
Demorar - To delay		
Terminar - To finish		
Pagar - To pay		

In Spanish, nouns are plural or singular as well as masculine or feminine. For example, the article "the" for Spanish, nouns ending with an *a*, *e*, and *i* (usually deemed as feminine) is typically *la*. For nouns ending with an *o*, or a consonant, then the noun is generally masculine, and the article is usually *el*. In plural form is *los* for masculine forms and *las* for feminine forms. "The boy" is *el* (the) *niño* (boy), "the girl" is *la niña*, "the boys" are *los niños*, and "the girls" are *las niñas*. ("the house" is *la casa*, "the car" is *el auto*). Although there are exceptions, such as for words that end with *ma*, *pa*, and *ta*, the article is usually *el*. Plus, some nouns are considered irregular and must be memorized. For example, "the problem" is *el problema* and not *la problema*. Also, the "wall" *la pared* or "the water" *el agua*.

For the article "a" (*un* and *una*), its conjugation is determined by feminine and masculine forms, "a car"—*un auto*, "a house"—*una casa*.

The conjugation for "this" (*esta*, *este*, *estos*, and *estas*) and "that" (*ese*, *esa*, *esos*, *esas*) is similar. "This," *este*, is masculine, for example, *este libro* ("this book"). Feminine is *esta*, for instance, *esta casa* ("this house"). *Estos libros* ("these books") and *estas casas* ("these houses") is the plural form. "That," *ese*, is masculine, that is, *ese libro* (that book). Feminine would be *esa*, for example, *esa silla* ("that chair"). In plural, this is *esos libros* ("those books) and *esas sillas* ("those chairs").

Temporary and Permanent

The different forms of "is" are *es* and *esta*. When referring to a permanent condition, for example, "she is a girl" (*ella es una niña*), you use *es*. For temporary positions, "the girl is doing well today" (*la chica esta muy bien hoy*), you use *esta*. However, *está* is also used to indicate a permanent location, for example, "Spain is located in Europe" / *España está ubicada en Europa*.

"You are" or "are you" could be translated as *estas*, or they could also be translated as *tú eres*. An example of temporary position is "how are you today?" (*cómo estas hoy*). And another example of temporary position is "you are here" (*estas aquí*). Another example of permanent position is "are you Mexican?" (*tú eres Mexicano?*) as well as "you are a man!" (*tú eres un hombre!*). Both derive from the verbs *ser* (permanent) and *estar* (temporary).

* **"I am"—*estoy* and *yo soy*.** *Yo soy* refers to a permanent condition: "I am Italian" / *Yo soy Italiano*. Temporary condition would be "I am at the mall" / *Estoy en el mall*.

* **"We are"—*somos* (permanent) and *estamos* (temporary).** *Somos Peruvianos* / "we are Peruvian" and *estamos en el parque* / "we are at the park."

* **"They are"—*son* (permanent)** *ellos son Chilenos* / "they are Chileans", **and estan (temporary)** *ellos estan en el auto* / "they are in the car."

Eso and *esto* are neuter pronouns, meaning they don't have a gender. They usually refer to an idea or an unknown object that isn't specifically named, for example, "that"/ *eso*; "that is"/ *eso es*;"because of that" / *por eso*; "this" / *esto*; "this is good" / *esto es bien;* and "what is this?" / *qué es esto?*

In regards to "my," singular and plural form exists as well, *mi* and *mis*.

* "my chair" / *mi silla*
* "my chairs" / *mis sillas*

With regard to "your," *tu* and *tus*, the singular is *tu*, as in *tu auto* / "your car," and the plural is *tus* (e.g., *tus autos* / your cars).

Verb Conjugation

The word "I" (*yo*) before a conjugated verb isn't required. For example, *yo necesito saber la fecha* ("I need to know the date") can be said, *Necesito saber la fecha* because *necesito* already means "I need" in conjugated form, although saying *yo* isn't incorrect! The same can also be said with *tú* / *te, el* / *ella, nosotros, ellos* / *ellas*, in which they aren't required to be placed prior to the conjugated verb, but if they are, then it isn't wrong.

Synonyms and Antonyms

There are three ways of describing time.

Vez/veces—"first time" / *primera vez* or "three times" / *tres veces*

Tiempo—"during the time of the dinosaurs" / *durante el tiempo de los dinosaurios*

Hora— "What time is it?" / *Qué hora es?*

Que has four definitions.

"What"—*Que es esto?* / "What is this?"

"Than"—*Estoy mejor que tu* / "I am better than you"

"That"—"I want to say that I am near the house" / *yo quiero decir que estoy acerca de la casa*

"I must" / "I have to"—*Tengo que*. The verb *tener*, "to have," whether it's in conjugated or infinite form, if it is followed by an infinitive verb, then *que* must always follow.

For example:

"I have to swim now" / *tengo que nadar ahora.*

There are two ways of describing "so."

"So"—*entonces*. "So I need to know" / *entonces necesito saber.*

"So"—*tan. Eso es tan distante* / "this is so far"

Si and Sí

Si (without accent) means "if"

Sí (with accent) means "yes"

Tú, Te, Ti and Tu

There are three different forms of how to use the pronoun "you"—*tú, te,* and *ti.*

Tú is a subject pronoun (second person of singular), referring to the individual who is doing the action. Unlike in English, it isn't required in Spanish. For example, in "you are here" / *estas aquí*, you aren't required to say *tú estas aquí*.

Te is a direct and indirect object pronoun, the person who is actually affected by the action that is being carried out. But the *te* comes before the verb, for example, "I send you" / *Yo te mando* or "I permit you" / *Yo te permito*. In the event the verb is infinitive, then *te* precedes the verb. For example, in the sentence "I want to follow you" / *quiero seguirte*, *seguir* and the *te* will connect with the verb and become one word.

Ti is a preposition pronoun, meaning it goes with a preposition (like *para, de, por*), for example, *para ti* / "for you" or *yo voy a ti* / "I am going to you" (added *a ti*).

Tu without the accent (´) means "your": *tu casa* / "your house."

Tuyo means "yours" and *tuyos* is plural, for example, *el libro es tuyo* / "the book is yours" and "the books are yours" / *los libros son tuyos*.

Ir a + *infinitive and* yo voy *&* me voy

In Spanish "to," *a* (pronounced as "ha"), isn't required between the conjugated verb and the infinitive form. For example, *Yo puedo decir* ("I can say"). But in regards to the verb "to go", *ir*, then the preposition *a* must always follow the *ir*, (whether in the conjugated or infinitive form) before connecting with the infinitive verb. For example, *Yo voy a ver* ("I am going to see") or *Yo necesito ir a buscar* ("I need to go to search"). "I go" and "I am going" could either be translated as *yo voy* or *me voy*. *Yo voy* refers to going to a specific place, for example, *yo voy a la tienda* ("I am going to the store"). *Me voy* is going somewhere and not specifying the exact destination, for example, *me voy afuera* ("I am going outside").

Using *De*

De is one of the most crucial prepositions in the Spanish language. Its most common use is much like the English words "from" and "of," but you will encounter it in other situations as well. It could also mean "than," "in," "with," and "by."

Use *de* when referring to "of" and "from."
   * "I am from the United States" / *soy de los Estados Unidos*.
   * "three more days of summer" / *tres más días de verano*.

Another form of *de* is to indicate the possessor.

   * *la casa de Moises* / "Moises's house" or "the house of Moises"
   * *las playas de Florida* / "Florida's beaches" or "the beaches of Florida"

Another use for *de* is for preposition phrases.

   * *afuera de la casa de tu novia* / "outside the house of your girlfriend"
   * *a lado de tu novio* / "next to your boyfriend"
   * *alrededor de la picina* / "around the pool"

However, if *de* is followed by *el* then both words combine to form *del*. For example, "from the car" / *del auto,* and **not** *de el auto.*

This should cover the most typical uses of *de.* However, there are other uses which haven't been mentioned here.

Using Lo *and* La

Lo and *La* are used as direct masculine, feminine, and neuter object pronouns, meaning "him," "her," or "it."

In case the verb is conjugated, *lo* and *la* precede the conjugated verb.

* "I don't want him to know" / *no lo quiero conocer*
* "I don't need her" / *No la necesito*

If the verb is in the infinitive form, then the *lo* and the *la* precede the infinitive verb and connect, creating one word:

* "I want to buy it." / *Quiero comprarlo.*
* "I want to find it." / *Quiero encontrarlo.*
* "I want to see her." / *Quiero verla.*
* "I don't want to know him." / *No quiero conocerlo.*
* "I don't want to give her." / *No quiero darla.*

Another example of using *lo* in Spanish, is, as the abstract neuter article "the".

* "the best of Charlie Chaplin" / *lo mejor de Charlie Chaplin* (since "best" is the abstract neuter noun).

Reflexive Form

In the Spanish language we use *me, te,* and *se* in relation to the reflexive form of a verb, which will be preceding or proceeding that verb, and set as a prefix or suffix. For example, the verb "to wash" - *lavar.*

"I wash myself" - *me lavo,*
"you wash yourself" - *te lavas,*
"he washed himself" - *se lava.*

In the infinitive form it connects as a suffix:
"I want to wash myself" - *quiero lavarme,*
"you wash yourself" - *quieres lavarte,*
"he washed himself" - *quiere lavarse.*

Conclusion

You have now learned a wide range of sentences in relation to a variety of topics such as the home and garden. You can discuss the roof and ceiling of a house, plus natural disasters like hurricanes and thunderstorms.

The combination of sentences can also work well when caught in a natural disaster and having to deal with emergency issues. When the electricity gets cut you can tell your family or friends, "I can only light this candle now." As you're running out of the house, remind yourself of the essentials by saying, "I need to bring my keys with me."

If you need to go to a hospital, you have now been provided with sentences and the vocabulary for talking to doctors and nurses and dealing with surgery and health issues. Most importantly, you can ask, "What is the emergency number in this country?" When you get to the hospital, tell the health services, "The hurricane caused a lot of destruction and damage in its path," and "We used the hurricane shelter for refuge."

The three hundred and fifty words that you learned in part 1 should have been a big help to you with these new themes. When learning the Spanish language, you are now more able to engage with people in Spanish, which should make your travels flow a lot easier.

Part 3 will introduce you to additional topics that will be invaluable to your journeys. You will learn vocabulary in relation to politics, the military, and the family. The three books in this series all together provide a flawless system of learning the Spanish language. When you visit Spain or Latin America you will now have the capacity for greater conversational learning.

When you proceed to Part 3 you will be able to expand your vocabulary and conversational skills even further. Your range of topics will expand to the office environment, business negotiations and even school.

Please, feel free to post a review in order to share your experience or suggest feedback as to how this method can be improved.

NOTE FROM THE AUTHOR

Thank you for your interest in my work. I encourage you to share your overall experience of this book by posting a review. Your review can make a difference! Please feel free to describe how you benefited from my method or provide creative feedback on how I can improve this program. I am constantly seeking ways to enhance the quality of this product, based on personal testimonials and suggestions from individuals like you. In order to post a review, please check with the retailer of this book.

Thanks and best of luck,

Yatir Nitzany